Braves' Banner 2015

MWES Writing Anthology 2014-2015

Writing pieces presented by the students of Mt. Washington Elementary School

Cover artwork by Jackson Cochran, 1st Grade

BLACK BOX PUBLISHING

Published by Black Box Publishing Company

ISBN# 978-0692448939

Printed in the United States of America

This publication was made possible by L. Henry Dowell and The Black Box Publishing Company.

Edited by Kelsey Shea

Contents

Narratives:

Informational:

<u>Poetry:</u>

Letters to Mrs. Lewis:

Stories/Fables/Legends:

Best Day of My Life

By: Savannah Fogle

It was a beautiful day to go swimming in the afternoon. My grandma took me to the public pool and I felt cheerful. It was the first time I went into the deep end. The sun shinned on me.

I went to the snack bar to get a drink of water and some chips. Then I went to the water sprinkler. I was in the sprinkler for one hour. It was almost time to go home. The crystal blue water shimmered in the pool. My grandma said, "We'll be back tomorrow." I then said with my happy voice, "OK." We each said good-bye.

On the next day we went to the public pool again. I wore a green bikini and my grandma wore a blue and purple bathing suit dress. The sun was brighter than a flash light. My grandma said, "10 more minutes." I said, "OK." It was time to go. Bye everyone. We said.

We came back again and the deep end was 10ft deep. At first I was in the shallow end. Then I swam to the rope that split up the shallow and deep end. Finally I was under the rope swimming to the deep end. "I did it" "Yay" My grandma said. I got out and got on the diving board. I dived in.

"Splash!" "You have 15 more minutes." "Let's go now so we can go eat dinner." I said, "OK." And we left. Bye every one.

I felt happy that my Grandma took me to the public pool. It was the best day of my life!

Broken knee

By: Josie Wood

One time 8 years ago my sister Kaylin was playing basketball. She was 14. She was about to shoot the ball but a girl pushed her forcefully out of the way. And she fell on the ground. My sister broke her knee.

After that she worked at ups and then some how she broke her knee again! Then she got it broke again! Now for 4 months she can't work at ups. She's actually happy because her feet hurt working there. She has to go fix her knee in 1 or 2 months. And after she gets her knee fixed I think she's going to cry!

Right now her knee might be aching, struggling and all that stuff. Right now she might be moving and struggling with her leg right now. I feel bad, terrible for her. I wish very, very much that her knee was not broken. Right now her knee must feel gross and yucky. My sister does a lot for me. She is my really, really good friend and my awesome BFF.

Halloween

By:Emma Steier

It was in the morning of Halloween just at sun rise and I had to watch everyone go to school. I got up seven times to puke. I puked stomach acid, it was not fun! I told my mom, "I hate Halloween so much." I went trick or treating for a little bit. I got sick a few time. I was Lady Gaga, going on a skiing trip for Halloween. It hailed frozen rain "perfect, for my costume!" It was a bad day to go trick or treating. Well that's what I said, because the sky was as black as it could be. You could not see the sun or the moon. Some tall teen agers came and I felt embarrassed at the moment. The girls were dressed up in old lady costumes and the boys weren't in a costume. There were six teens it was scary. They left at me because I was small. I felt totally sad!

And now it was in the middle of the night. We got to stay up all and watch movies all night and I still hate Halloween you can't change my mind. So now do you know why I hate Halloween? In my heart I know it will happen again, well it happens every year.

MY FIRST BASKETBALL POINTS

By Austin Jones

It was a hot Sunday morning and I was still in bed. My mom woke me at 8:00 in the hot morning. And she said Austin it is Sunday! I said "so what". She said today you have your big smooth basketball game today. And I am like shout I have to get ready super-fast. And mom said no doubt. I asked dad did you get my cloths out last night. And he said "no I forgot" and I said "ok I can get them myself". And so he said "do you no everything you have to get". And I said "no I do not know everything I am supposed to wear". And he said "ok I will come and help you". And so I said out loud "THANK YOU"!!!!!!!!! . So I got out what I knew I had to wear and he got out the rest out. So I say mom what basketball shoes am I wearing today? And she said you are wearing your blue basketball shoes today. Why Because today is a big day. So she says yes of course I said ok.

So I get my clothes off and then I get my basketball cloths on. And then I put my shoes out in front of the counter. Mom says dad can you get cadent out of his bed. He said ok. Mom said Austin I need you to get your shoes on. And so I said "can I see caden" and she said "sure yes you can" and I said "thank you". And then mom said "get in the car". And we said "ok" to me it sounded like to me it was forever. And then we got to the basketball court we were warming up.

And then it was time for the game .We got the basketball first and in the 4th Quarter I got the basketball and took a shot and I got fouled and the reef said 2!!!! Shots so I went to the line but I missed the first one but that was ok and I made the second one and we won the game and the court was very smooth. After the game the team had a really good talk finally we got to go home I got my clothes off .And then I had a chance to play with my little brother. And that was the best day of my life. And when I sat on the couch it felt ruff and bumpy. And when I was playing with cadenes toys. It felt really smooth.

And then it was time for bed I was so tired I could not rests it. And then I woke up the next day and we had a snow day. I got to play in the snow it was soggy and soft. And I came in and I felt warm and cozy.

My First Pet Turtle

By: Travis Meyer

It was a sunny afternoon. Me and my dad where in the woods And I said " dad look" and there was a turtle and we named it Mashell Anglow. Later , me and dad got home we fed it and we gave Mashell some water in a bowl And finally Mashell went to sleep.

Then the next day me and dad and my brother went to the pet store and got some more food for Mashell. We looked around and Finally we found the isle and we found great food for Mashell. Then we got home And we fed it to Mashell and she drank some water. We got home and poured the Water into Mashell's water bowl and we gave Mashell the food. She drank some of the water and some of the food too. And it went to sleep and the next day we looked at Mashell and all of her food was gone and water too. I said, "where is Mashell's food and water?" and I poured some more water and gave her more water and gave her more food in her bowl she was still asleep. I told mom and dad and my brother too.

And later then I was looking if Mashell was awake and she was not awake. Later then I looked again and she was awake and she was went back to sleep. I said " why would she go back to sleep when you are awake that makes no sense!"

The next morning we saw that all Mashell's food was still there and her water. "last time there was none there!" We digged up worms so she ate the worms and ate some of her food. It was only one day later when Mashell died. I feeled sad because she was my first pet. My brother buried her. He digged a tiny hole because her shell was not as big as a basketball. “We’re gonna love her”.

MY FIRST ROLLER COASTER

By: Jay Monks

It was 9.00pm and my mom woke me up and said, "It is time to go to Disney world!" We went to the car so I fell asleep in the car. I knew that Disney World was a long time for my house so I went to bed.

I woke up saw Disney world and said, "Do you have jet packs on your car?" My mom laughed then got out. My mom bumped right after me. I was looking and looking but I could not find the biggest roller coaster but just kept walking. But I stop the longs walk in my life. It was the biggest roller coaster I have EVER SEEN farther then I can see and it was big as a 100 foot giant and long as a 300 foot python! It was the best roller coaster and longest.

I would rather be at Disney world instead of 1,000 birthday parties where I got so many presents it would fill up my whole house. Finally, I got home at 8:00 my parents said, "Did you have fun?" I said, "yes! It was the best day of my life!" When I went to bed I was as tired as a bear ready to hibernate that is covered in blankets. I cannot wait to do it again!

My Grandma Died

By: Leland Stafford

It was an early sunny Tuesday. I was going to my Grandma's yellow house and I was feeling really happy.

And when we got there we saw my Grandma in her flower dress and white hair. My Dad rolled her over there was blood coming out of her mouth. She had tried to get in her bed but her legs hurt bad and her legs weren't working. Nobody was helping her. I bet she had pain.

My Dad called 911 and the hospital came. My Dad told me to go wait in the car. I sat there alone and he came to check on me. My Mom came and took me to my Grandpa's. My cousin came. My heart was beating fast and I couldn't breathe because my tears were coming out. It felt like a long car ride.

My white furred cat made me feel happy and I stopped crying. The cat was chasing the laser pointer and it was hilarious.

I hope she's having a happy time dancing in heaven. Maybe now she can cause there's no pain.

Perfect North

By:Adam McGoff

It was a late winter afternoon and we got stuck in traffic that makes you feel crazy. Then a girl bumped in to us. When she bumped in to us it did not hurt our car because we had a trailer hook but she had a dent on her car.

Then we finally got there. My mom, sister and my sister's friend went somewhere. Me and my dad snow boarded on a gigantic hill as tall as two houses put on top of each other! I went super-fast! I had to crash because couldn't go straight down! There was rock right in front of us! I landed on my face a couple of times! It gave me a burn!

We all ended up snowboarding. We went home and there was no traffic! I thought-whoa! That's weird! Our trip to Perfect North was one of the best times of my life!

Sleepover

By: Jessica Browne

It was 4 o'clock in the afternoon I had a sleep over first when I got home from the grocery I went on the trampoline with winter. We played on until every body got here and when even body got here except for one person.

We all started to eat pizza I had a meat lovers and then Tammy got here We all had pizza and then we played and then we made crafts.

We Made baby blankets and that was herd. And then we made necklaces But we did not make bracelets.

Next we played limbo and Jaylen Bumped her head on the TV. I said just don't dance.

And then we All watched dolphin tale 2 and we when to bed at an 11.00. The Next morning we hit Tammy with pillow and when my mom got Up she said it is time for breakfast and after that everyone went home.

I felt really happy that everyone enjoyed my party. They enjoy what My mom set up and she did it for me and my friends to make us happy.

Texas

By: Trinity Ritchey

It was winter when I went to Texas. I was wearing blue jeans and a pink shirt to see my grandparents first time ever. I went on a airplane with Calin and grandma hearting.

When we got off the airplane we walked to the house. Jason opened the door that is my daddy's little brother. I watched TV.

Suddenly grandma walked in the door. She was wearing a black suit and sunglasses. She said "hi Trinity. I missed you." I stayed there for a week. In the pass week I spilled a lot of coke.

When I left I said "I will see you again." And she came back but this time she came to Kentucky. I feel happy when I am with her.

The Close Sting Ray

By : Dayne Barnett

It was a hot summer day. I was the first one to go in the ocean. Then a half-hour later, I said to myself, Time to get back on the beach. I made a 15 minute sand castle.

After the 15 minutes, I went back in the ocean. The red flag was up. My mom yelled, "Dayne! There's a sting ray behind you!" I yelled, "Mom, help." But she was too scared to help. I was thinking he's an inch away from me. Then, my mom said, Time to go back to the hotel. I was so happy. My feet were covered in wet white sand. I liked the big blue ocean. I did **not** like the brown sting ray.

When we arrived it was normal. The red sky was setting. The sun was orange-ish yellow-ish. The next day, I woke up. The sand color changed. The sand was yellow. I look at the beautiful jelly fish. Their color was purple and pink. The sting ray was laying there to get more energy. He slept there so I would come again. The same thing happened to me from yesterday. The sting ray was red-ish brown-ish. Those are the friendly ones.

It was dark, and hot, hot afternoon in Florida. I was comfortable at 8:30pm I fell on the bed, and I went to sleep. It was pretty amazing!

The First Time I Ride a Roller Coaster

By: Paul Harris

It was early in the morning. Me and my mom were up waiting for the park to open. It was cold out. The air was calm and it made a noise like a bird song. We were the first ones to get there.so we had to wait a long time. Finally the gates opened and we got the first tickets like a king getting a crown. It was glorious. Then we ride a ride. Then we came to the big roller costar it looked scary it was as tall as a castle I said" mom I don't want to go on this ride" but I did and it was fun and I ride it again and my blue shirt made the roller costar look blue the roller costar hade stripes like thunder

I felt happy I would like to go to the park again and my mouth was so cold that I count not tell her that I loved the day

The Worst Day of My Life Time

By: Carson Luttrell

It was past noon and when the sun sets when I was playing tag with my friends. And all of a sudden I saw a red spot on the carpet and stopped for a moment.

We looked around for a second and then we saw 5 more drops of red stuff. I said to myself,''could it be blood?'' Then the whole space was absorbed of red stuff and that's when we knew it was blood!

My face was covered in it! The gash was by my eye! We got in the car's seats. I was begging my dad to not have to go to the hospital. I didn't know what it felt like to get stitches.

We sped over to the emergency center. I got stitches. It felt like I was dying. I was in a lot of pain. I said,"No,No,No" in a scared way.' I saw an evil person in a white coat trying to hurt me. But after it was over and a few hours past and I didn't feel it. It was the worst day of my life time!

When I Can Swim Without Floaties

By: Delilah Seay

It was a hot sunny day in June and I and my cousins were swimming until it was time for dinner. But I and my cousins stayed at the pool. So we decided to stay at the pool because we already ate dinner.

Then my cousin Jaiden said "Do you want to see if you can swim without floaties?" And I said "yeah" So when I reached level ten my heart was beating full of bravery .A few moments later I did it! I reached the end of the pool! So Jaiden and Lark were cheering for joy and they told the family and they were very proud of me, especially my mom because she knew I can do it!

"And when I jumped in it kind of changed colors" And I said to my mom "and the wind is so strong I didn't think I would make it" "Will all you got to do is follow your heart And believe yourself" My mom said. And the rest of the year that stuff that was challenging all you got to do is believe in yourself.

And that's what I even do now. And all you got to do if you're having a hard trying something like backbends and backflips even anything. And then I said “I like the way you said that”.

When I got My Awesome Dog!

By: Caylie Gore

It was early Saturday and the sun wasn't up yet. Me and my awesome family were going to my aunt's beautiful home for Christmas.

After a great yummy feast we opened our presents the paper was shinny and pretty. When we opened our last present it was...dog toys and a gray dog bed. We said "huh?" I was shocked.

Then a white dog with soft silky hair came from down stairs! We were so excited. I screamed! So we went home and played fetch with our dog and named him Gizmo. We had dinner and we played lots more.

Around 10 o'clock at night we said, "we are so tired!" So we went to bed. That day was great! We had so much fun with our new white and brown dog Gizmo!

When I Jumped Off a Cliff

By:Avery Hallinan

One Saturday it was sticky hot. I was riding back on the red pontoon back to the camper and we stopped at a cliff and my dad said, "Do you want to jump off a cliff with me?" I said "No, I am eating!" My dad said, "Are you sure?" "Ok I will do it'' I said.

I got out of the boat with my mom and I climbed up the hill! My eyes were getting waterey .I got really scared I hugged a tree! Finally we got to the top of the windy hill! My mom said "Are you ready?'' "Yes," I said bravely!

Then I jumped off the high cliff! The green water shimmered underneath me. My heart was racing like a roller coaster. I hit the water and I was under water for a second. I faced my fear and it was fun! "Dad, can you help me up?" He said, "I'll do anything for you, princess!"

Then we rode back on the boat. You should never be afraid to do scary things because if you are you'll never do anything awesome the rest of your life.

When I Lost the Championship

by: Trey Woods-Patrick

It was a hot day outside in July. I played for the Mount Washington all-stars. On the first day we played two games. We won both.

Then on the next day we were going to play two games. But on the first, game there was a delay. So when my team was in the dugout one of the umps said we made it to the championship. So the championship game was on a Tuesday. But there was a delay. So the make-up game was on a Wednesday.

In the championship we lost bot we still got a trophy. My heart was beeping really fast when I heard that my team was moving on to the championship. The trophy was brown small, and cool. The look on my face looked like yah, yah, yah. That was a special day for me.

When I Rode My Bike For the First Time

By: Lukas Staab

One late evening me and my dad were learning how to ride my bike. I was scared at the beginning. My dad held the back pushing it. I dragged my feet before I hit the mailbox. It felt hard.

Then I did it! I knew how to ride my bike! My bike is red. Then I said to myself I did an awesome job! Even my dad said I did an awesome job too! I knew I could do it every time! When we got in the house I told my mom and she was so exited! My mom is pretty. She's proud of me! And I was never afraid!

When My Dog Died

By Maison Weekley

One day when I came home from school at noon I opened the door and as I stepped in I saw blood very where there was ever, blood on the walls on the door and on the floor. I got really curious. My dad told my dog had a very bad nose bleed.

Later that night me and my mom put my dog Halley in the garage on her bed with my rainbow blanket and went to bed. As soon as I woke up my dad told me that Halley died, I busted into tears as I cried loudly. It was hard to get ready to go to school that morning.

When I got to school I told my friends that my dog died that night and that my dad told me my dog named Halley died. I was sad that because my own friends did not care about what I said or what happened to my dog Halley.

She was a good dog. I loved her and she loved me.

Jellyfish Problem

By: Lilly Leveronne

On a hot summer morning as are ship arrived at Disney privet island ,my dad was preparing for a 5k so me and my bonus mom Briley went to go get our friends from a nearby room. We headed to the beach! I went into the ocean and I felt something touch me but then all the sudden red spots stared popping everywhere I thought to myself, well surely I am imagining !" But no I was not imagining! My daddy took a picture with our water proof camera when he got back from the 5k then we figure out that it was a jellyfish sting! It burned like a sizzling of a fire! Briley went to go to get a person that worked there to see if they knew what to do and the lady said ," hot water helps "! as she handed her the cup. We ran to the bathroom .I said ,"all better " as she poured the hot water on my blood red spots on my legs and arms. Later that day we rented bicycle, swam, and had dinner at nemo's palace. It was late past my bedtime when we went back to our room. As we got all snug in our beds, I was out like a light! I thought to myself as I fell asleep "what a jellyfish day!"

My New Dog

By Joshua Jones

It was 5:00 at night and the sun was setting and it was very beautiful. We were going to a person's house to see our new dogs eyes open. We were driving. We were looking to see where we should eat after we saw the dog's eyes. There were lots of restaurants to choose from. I asked "when will we get there" probley in ten minutes .Jakob woke up and Jakob said" where are we" dad said "we are almost there" we were turning a lot when we were near.

When we get there we heard a lot of barking behind and beside the house. We knocked on the white door and two old people came to the front door and said "come in". When we walked in the house it was brown and it looked like it was very old. The old man walked away to get the dog. And my mom and dad where talking to the woman.

A few minutes later the man walked in the room and put the little dog on the table and the dog was black with a big white spot on its neck and its feet were white to. The dog's fur was silky soft like a pillow. The dog played with its toy monkey and a few minutes past and it fell asleep. A few minutes went by and we bot the dog and then we left the brown and reddish house. And went to the back yard and saw! To adult corgis and a pug the pug was barking and the corgis weren't barking and the pug bit me and my brother then we left.

The Day at the Beach

By: Ava Smith

It was a hot sunny day in the afternoon.me and my family was at the sandy beach it was really fun. But I was scared of the water. I only played in the sand with my sister Olivia. That was really fun then I walked close to the water. Then I notice that I was in the water.

Then my dad said come to the deep end. No I'm really scared I thought in my brain. Then my dad walked closer to me then he picked me up. Then he put me at the deep end of the ocean. It was up to my chest. I stayed in the ocean for a while and then I finally got used to it more. Then my dad did not tell me there were sharks in the ocean.

So then I got out of the ocean I went sand and made a sand castle. The sand was really hot. My mom and dad told me to come back into the ocean. I said I don't think that's a very good idea. 'my mom said,' come on only for a few minutes.' I said I guess so. ok. Let's go jump over the waves with daddy and Olivia. Ok let's go this is really fun I love this beach.' My mom said me too. What else do you want to do, let's go play in the sand? Ok I made a sand castle. Cool. the sand was getting all over me on my purple bathing suit. My sister said, I went under the waves with daddy.

We jumped over the waves together and that was really fun. My dad said, let's go we have been out here for a long time.' We went back to the hotel I really didn't want to leave but I was really tired. It was the most special day ever.

Through the Haunted Forest

I went to Jelly stone and I went to the haunted forest. I went through it with daddy ty, and papa Tom. We stood in a long line. We heard people scream. We also hard chainsaws and it made me nervous. We stood in a long line. It took about 30 minutes. It was cold. Then we went through it. Then this guy came out of nowhere and had a chainsaw. Then this clown came and said **boo** and did a scary laugh. Finally we were getting close to the end. As we were leaving we saw a boy cutting a girl's hand off. We were getting lost. I was cold I was scared but excited and happy we went through it all. I hope you had fun hearing about my life at Jelly Stone.

By: Payton Patterson
Ms. Sizemore's Class
1st Grade
January 30, 2015

Victory Is Ours

I am going to tell you about when I won all six basketball games. My coach taught me how to shuffle. I learned how to dribble. Our team's offense and defense was strong. Our coach was a good teacher. Our teams received medals .I was happy that my team won all six games. I hope you enjoyed hearing about my basketball team.

By: Barrett Armstrong
Ms. Sizemore's Class
1st Grade
February 6, 2015

My Trip to Chicago

*2015 District Young Authors Finalist, 1st Grade

I went to Chicago with my Nanna, Rose Mary and my friend El. We went in the American girl store. El and I got to pick out an American girl doll. We had dinner in American girl store. My American girl doll had red curly hair her name was Ally she had blue eyes freckles. El's doll had blond straight hair, freckles, and blue eyes .The next day we all went on a Ferris wheel. The first time around El and I were nervous. The Ferris wheel was slow. Then after first time on the Ferris wheel El and I got used to it. El and I got to go on a pirate ship we got to raise the sails we got to eat chips on the ship. On the ship we went all around the water. I hope you like learning about what I did in Chicago.

By: Kyla French
Ms. Sizemore's Class
1st Grade
February 6, 2015

My First 1st place win

By Alyssa Nourtsis

It was January 31st I went my first All Star cheer competition. My team is Bullitt Athletics Crystals. I am going to tell you about it.

It started out we were in the warm up room. We were in there for about an hour then we warmed up. We warmed up stunts and tumbling first. Last before we competed we warmed up our full out routine.

And then we competed I was so scared. We did everything correct and how it was suppose to be. Then we waited another hour or so for awards to start.

The last part of the competition was the awards. Before I knew it they called us the youth prep level one division which was me. They called 3rd which was not us then 2nd which was not us . I was so excited that our team had not been called. Last they called1st place in the youth prep level one division Bullitt Athletics Crystals. My whole team started jumping and screaming. We got a medal and a team trophy for the gym and best of all a bid to The U.S. Finals.

That was all about my first 1st place win in my first All Star cheer competition. I hope It was exciting.

My Poor Doggy!

One wintery evening I came home. I had a wonderful day at school although I was still thinking about my dog because she had been in the animal hospital. I rushed inside hoping Maddie was there, but instead she was still in the hospital and she was very sick.

Later that night mom came home. She was crying. She told us that Maddie died. I started to cry into my dad's arm. He always makes me feel better when I'm really sad. He said," get some water and you can sleep with mommy tonight!" I said "ok, I love you" I got one last drink of water then headed off to bed with mommy. She was my whole world I didn't know what I would do without her.

Even though two weeks has passed, my other dog, Peyton, and I are still upset about losing our best friend. Peyton has started whining now that she realizes Maddie is gone. But now I'm getting used to having only one pet. I want to keep Maddie's memory with us, so I still have a stuffed animal that looks like her. Maddie was a dirty blonde yorkie with a mini brown nose and little rich pink ears! She was soooooo cute! She wore little sweaters when she was cold. I still have memorys of last Christmas when Peyton got a huge bone and Maddie dragged it around the house! She was my sweet little baby.

Now you can see I love my doggy, and I miss Mo-Mo (Maddie)! But she will always be in my heart!

By Kadence Owen
Grade 3

My Christmas Gift

I was asleep on Christmas morning and I had a dream about what Santa would bring me. It reminded me that today was Christmas! I instantly woke up and woke my sisters up by saying "Wake up its Christmas." in a quiet shout. Then my sisters Emily and Madelyn and I went to my moms and dads room and on the way there my sisters and I saw presents on the floor by our Christmas tree. There were 2 tablets and an American girl doll with a bunch of outfits.

The doll had long blond hair, white skin, and was born in 1974 her name is Julie. I wanted the doll but also wanted a tablet. Then I thought that I have one and so does Madelyn. So I let Emily have the doll since she does not have one. After giving the doll away there were the 2 tablets left. There was a pink one and a purple one. I said "I want the pink one!" So Madelyn got the purple one. I was so enthusiastic that I immediately grabbed it and started downloading music.

My parents came into the living room so we opened the presents. I was so excited when I opened one present I got from my mom. It was a charming outfit that said sassy on the side of the pants and it was Minney Mouse on the shirt. I also got a book called Mouse Heart. Before Christmas I begged my mom to get me that book. I was so delighted I got Mouse Heart. I was so joyful of what I got for Christmas from my mom most of all!

I bet my dog had a good Christmas too because my fluffy brown and black dog, Toby, got about six toys and a very soft bed to put in his cage. Now he can be cozy at night when he is in his cage. I thought that he was a pretty lucky dog. Don't you?

That was an insane Christmas. Don't you think so? Well I think so! I got everything I wanted but the thing that was my best loved was my outfit from my mom!!!

By Samantha Sadolsky
Grade 3
Mrs. Dixon

The Longest Road Trip Ever

We all got in the slate, silver car to drive to Disney World on the Friday before spring break. You probably think that the drive down was the easy part. Well, it wasn't.

My dad woke me up and said, "Get up! Time for the trip"! I was so enthusiastic, I could barely stay still!

I was extremely tired, because I got up at 7:00 in the morning. "Mom, can I take a nap in the car? Please?" I said in a very weak voice. "It won't be too long till we will arrive at IHOP". My mom said. I NEVER liked IHOP at all, but we went there anyway and we all had a good time.

We left at about 8:00 in the morning and I was so happy. When we left IHOP and we got back in the car and I took a long nap.

After that, we still had about 10 hours left. My brother, Thomas, started kicking me for about 30 minutes. "Mom, tell Thomas to stop now!" I screamed in such a loud voice that even the people in the car beside us looked at me. After that was over I watched The Sound of Music, Jimmy Neutron, Frozen and Monster High. To watch the movies we used little TV's on the back of my mom and dad's seat's that were charcoal black for the case.

We drove all day long until we began to feel miserable and sleepy. Mom suggested we stop to stay in a hotel. You would think that was easy, right? But, NO! Mom called almost every hotel in town. Finally, she called and found a vacant room. Once we arrived, we had to unload a ton of suitcases and bags and carry them through the pouring down rain. As soon as we got to our room we put away a few things and jumped into bed.

The next morning we woke up, packed our luggage, and rushed to the elevator. It was time for the breakfast buffet. After quickly eating we ran outside to get back on the road with just an hour left on our road trip to Disney World!

At last, we got there and had a lot of fun. We went to Animal Kingdom, Magic Kingdom and Hollywood Studios. Even though our trip there was the hardest, it was still a beyond awesome vacation!

Written by Jenna Sherrard
Third Grade
Mrs. Dixon

A Memory in a Necklace

by Kyla Combs

Once my grandma had a necklace. It was magenta and blue and really sparkly. I really wanted it, but every time I asked, she would say, "NO." It had a picture of me and her in it when we were at the zoo. As years passed, she got older. I would still ask her but she would still say, no because the necklace was a memory to her. I would still ask her for the necklace, but she said when I die I will tell your mom to give the necklace to you.

I was so excited when she said I could have it, but I thought it wouldn't be for a while. Well, I was wrong. The next day she started feeling all woozy and lost her mind a few times. We took her to the hospital and found out she had brain cancer. She only spent a few months alive. My grandma gave me the necklace before she went to bed one night. In the morning she wouldn't wake up. I heard my grandpa and mom in the bedroom crying she had died right there in the living room. I looked at the necklace and started to cry.

When I went to the mass at church, I took a good look at the necklace and started to cry. The next day at Sunday dinner I kept on glancing at the necklace every five minutes. After dinner, I made a soda float and accidently dropped the necklace in it!

I had to quickly fish it out! As soon as I got it, I started to dry it and polish it and made sure it was ok, which it was. Now every time I look at the necklace I think of my grandma.

The Day I Got my Ears Pierced

I was getting my ears pierced at the beauty shop named Elite Creations. I went with my mommy. The lady who worked there her name was Angela. I went in there and I got in the big chair. Then she talked to me to make sure I wanted to get them pierced. First she cleaned them and then she took a marker and made x's on my ears. Then she put the earring in the gun. Next she cleaned them. Then she put the t gun up to my ears and they are now pierced. I hope you like reading about when I got my ears pierced.

By: Tabatha Lewis
Ms. Sizemore's Class
1st Grade
January 30, 2015

Plane

First I first flew on a plane and I flew to Texas. Next I was with my mom and Aunt Emily. I liked when I flew on the plane. We bumped when we landed. Also it tickled my belly when we went up. We hand fun on the plane. We played flash cards and listened to music. Afterwards we got a snack and a drink. I got pretzels, peanuts, and a sprite. I loved flying on the plane. I hope you learned what it is like to fly on a plane.

By: Caroline Nethery
Ms. Sizemore's Class
1st Grade
January 30, 2015

My Papaw!

By Lilly Rhoades

I want to tell you about my Papaw. My Papaw loved me , was very happy and so special to me! My Papaw gave me a bracelet. My bracelet is a cinnamon color (like the color in my hair). It's almost a fancy watch/bracelet. I wear it almost every day. When I got it I said, "Thank you, I love it! "You're welcome. I'm glad you like it!" Grandpa said. I told him, "I love you!"

When I received the bracelet I was so happy and felt special and now I feel even more special, because right now he's in Heaven. I really miss him, but I know I have special memories in my heart that will always stay with me.

Looking back, in the summer my brother, cousins, Papaw and Mamaw and I always went to the pool together. It was always fun getting to go. A year later my Papaw died at the age of 65. My papaw died because of cancer. I'm not certain what kind he had, but I know it was cancer. I really miss him and I always will!!

My Daddy in the Hospital

By Ashley Love

It was a cold winter night and all of the snow was white and my daddy was in the hospital. My daddy's heart was not working. The Doctor had to give him exercise because he was chubby.

I knew he was in the hospital because my mommy told me. Then I went to the bedroom and I cried for a long time because my daddy was in the hospital I was sad. I ask my mommy "Is he going to die?" and she said I don't know.

Then my grandma came over to watch us then my mommy to see my daddy. Then my mommy came home and daddy came home to. I was so excited because he came home and he was okay to.

Sami

By Marley Long- Mrs. Perry's

When I was a baby, not even born, my mom had a baby shower for me. There were streamers in pink and white and so was everything else. There was a huge sign that read, It's A Girl! Everyone, even my mom's and dad's friends were excited about the baby. "I'm so excited!" blurted out my mom's friend, Nattily. "Me too!" screamed another one of my mom's friends. Soon, the whole room was repeating those words.

"Ladies and gentlemen!" mom warned everyone. "Time for food!" There was a huge, pink and white cake. Mom ate half the cake and her face was covered in icing. LOL! Finally, we started to open presents. I got a rattle, a blanket, even a sippy cup, but then, there was a blue, stuffed sloth sitting on a book called, ***Marley's Big Surprise***. The sloth was named Marley, like from the book.

Instead of Marley, I called him *Sami.* Now, to this day, he's on his own personal pillow, on my bed.

Going to Kentucky Kingdom

By: Coby Barnett

The first time I went to Kentucky Kingdom was when I was three. I rode rollercoasters, played fun games, and ate awesome food. I told my grandpa "That was so fun! I had a blast!"

On the way there, I would watch the trees go by and play road games. I only got to go to Kentucky Kingdom once. On the way, I kept asking, "Are we there yet? Are we there yet?" He said, "No." I kept repeating that the whole ride there. I was just so excited to get there! When I got there, I asked him "Can I have something to eat?" He said, "Not yet, because I have to pay first." Then when he paid to get in I started yelling, "Can I get food yet? Can I get food yet? He finally got me a hot dog and fries! YUM!

My grandpa was trying to get me to go on a big rollercoaster and I wouldn't. I was way too scared that I would fall off or out of it! You know, I've heard about things like that on the news! I rode a smaller rollercoaster and the smaller rollercoaster was not scary at all. There were a few bumps, but it wasn't scary. I also had fun playing games. We played several kinds and that was a blast!

After we left, my grandpa took me back to my house. It was fun at Kentucky Kingdom, but I was glad to be home!

So what do you think? Do you think it would be fun to go to Kentucky Kingdom? Thanks for reading.

The Storm

By: Jordan Powell

Once I had a flood. I was sitting on my couch I had asked my mom what is going on outside. She looked out the window and said we have a flood in our backyard. I heard a BOOM-the rain hitting the water. And I went to the back door, at the back door I felt water I looked down at the water it was hunter green.

Then I looked out the front door. I looked all the way down my neighborhood. I saw water all the way down the road. Then my toys came out of my play house my dad had to go get the toys. I was very scared until my dad said “It’s not very bad.”

After that, we drove down where people drive four-wheelers. There was a lot of water. Then we got in the bath tub. Then my dad went to look at the flood he said it’s not bad my mom started to cook again and my dad started to watch TV again when he said it was fine I yelled I was so happy because I love to play basketball when I got done I practice baseball when I got done I went to bed.

HOME-WORK

By: Jackson Hartlauf

Hello, I'm Jackson Hartlauf and I'm going to be talking about home-work. I think that home-work is necessary; because it makes you get a good future and a good job. So here we go!

First, home-work makes you smarter, so you can know math facts. Also, if your children want to know something, you can answer them. And it helps it helps you get a good job.

Also, home-work makes you get good grades. Witch getting good grades gives you a good collage. Also, by getting good grades in collage gets you a good life with a house and a job with food, children, pets, and a girlfriend witch turns in to your wife.

Finally, homework is for something to fill empty times instead of T.V. and video-games. It also it fills you brain with knowledge and smartness. So that is why I love homework.

In conclusion, I hope you liked my option about my awesome fabulous home-work; and all my facts about home-work. Also, there will be more home-work books coming to a library near you! Bye!

ROLLERCOASTER

By: Daniel Tharp – Mrs. Perry

I did something so crazy I rode a rollercoaster for my first time! It was called Space Mountain in Disney World. Next, I was in the seat and leaned over and said to my sister, "Taylor I am scared!" Taylor said, "It`s ok!" I said, "Can I get off and do something else?" My sister said, "Nope TOO LATE!" What was even worse, was the fact that we just had to sit in the front so the whole time I was screaming my head off!!! When I got off, I thought I was going to fall over! I was so dizzy!

After words, I stopped by a place called Felonies. After I ate, I got cotton candy. Then we went to Space Mountain again. I got on again, only me this time. I kind of liked it, but I still screamed really loud. I bet my mom and dad heard me thru the tunnel!! I could of done some of my little brother's rollercoasters, but mine were way cooler! After I found my mom and dad I said, "I had a blast!!!"

That was the best time I have ever had. I love riding rollercoasters and can't wait to go back to Disney World!

How to make a chicken burrito

By Jack Matthews

Ingredients
Chicken
Soft shell tortia
Sour cream

Utensils
Skillet
Fork
Toothpick

Steps

1. Put chicken on skillet (put skillet on the medium setting).

2. After the chicken is finished cooking put sour cream and chicken on tortia.

3. Roll up the tortia.

4. To keep the tortia closed put a toothpick in it.

Now you are Finished!

Dangerous tornados!

By: Zoe Thomas- Mrs. Perry's Class

What is one of the most dangerous kinds of weather on earth? Tornados! They're so strong, they can damage Earth's surface! I'm going to tell you about what Tornados are, how it changes the earth surface, and How the tornado got its name.

What is a tornado? What are tornados? These huge storms can be more than thousands of feet tall. Tornados are made from warm, cold, and dry air. As it gets closer, and closer to the ground, it spins faster, and faster! Some times when it gets big enough, it can make more of the tornado. A tornado is called a water spout.

How do they damage the earth? Tornados can kill more than 80 people each year. Tornados are very strong. They can pick up a tree, Or even a house! Water spouts can pick up animals In the water, once a water spout made it rain frogs in England! Tornados can suck you too! How did they get there name? Some people don't know how the tornado got its name. Some think it came from the Latin word "ton are." "Ton are", means to twist or spin. Other people call a tornado a twister. The eye of a tornado is a big hole in it.

Now, you have learned a lot of facts about what a tornado is, how they damage the earth, and how the tornado got its name.

Wampanoag House

I am going to tell you what it would be like living in a Wampanoag house. In a Wampanoag house it is very small and it is all in one room.

A Wampanoag house is called a wetu. There were baskets and bags hanging on the walls. There was a fire in the middle of the Wampanoag house to keep warm. The Wampanoag's also had a garden.

I hope you like learning about a Wampanoag's house.

By Kyla French
November 24, 2014
Ms. Sizemore's Class
Resources:
www.scholastic.com

Pilgrim House

I am going to tell you what it would be like if you lived in a pilgrim house. Everything was in one room and it was very crowded. The pilgrims moved furniture around a lot. They used a big pot to put over the fire and cook food. The pilgrims had a garden to plant food. They had oil lamps and no windows. I hope now you know how it was when they lived in a house.

By:Molly Priddy
Ms. Sizemore's Class
1st Grade
11.24.14
Resources:
www.scholastic.com

Cohen Miller

2nd Grade

Mrs. Cooper

Seed Dispersal

Animals help plants in many ways. One example of how animals help plants is they help move seeds to different spots. A bur has spikes on it to stick to other animals so they can move the seeds to new places. Another example of how animals help plants are when a squirrel buries a nut and it grows in to a tree.

The last example of how animals help plants are when an animal eats a berry and it comes out the back.

The scat gives the seed food. I hope you learned a lot about how animals help plants. For example, when an animal makes scat, hitching a ride like a bur and forgetting a seed was in the ground.

Tornado Facts

By: Coby Barnett

Goodness! That tornado is huge! Did you know that tornadoes mostly happen in the spring and summer? Did you know that a tornado is also a spinning funnel cloud? Did you know tornadoes also form when it's hot and cold? I am going to tell you other facts to.

Where Tornadoes Happen? Tornadoes can happen anywhere! They mostly happen in tornado alley. Tornado alley is in the central U.S. The place that has the most tornadoes is the U.S., every year they have thousands of tornadoes. Australia has the second most tornadoes every year. Tornadoes rarely happen in cold places but they still can happen.

How Do Tornadoes Form? Tornadoes form when hot and cold mix together. The cold air drops as the warm air rises. The warm air eventually twists into a spiral and forms a funnel cloud. The funnel cloud reaches lower and lower until it reaches the ground. The spinning funnel cloud keeps on damaging, and damaging stuff until it spins back into the sky. Yay!

Cleaning up after a Tornado People have to do a lot of cleaning up after a tornado.

The first step to cleaning up after a tornado is picking up all the stuff that it flung around. The second step to cleaning up after a tornado is wiping off everything that got dirt on it from the tornado. The final step of cleaning up after a tornado is building everything back. Cleaning up after a tornado is a lot of work but it's worth it.

No matter if you're talking about where tornadoes happen, or how they form, or cleaning up after a tornado what really matters is you staying safe.

Polar Bears

Hi my name is Ryan and I am going to teach you about Polar Bears. Does that sound fun? They live in the North Pole. Where in the North Pole? They live in a den in the North Pole. They have black big thick layers under their fur to keep them warm. They stay in the den and the den is very warm so that will help them stay warm to. They live in the Arctic and Arctic is a name for the North Pole. Babies will stay in the den with there mom and they will stay in there for two years. After the two years are over the baby Polar Bears will come out with their mom in the world. They will not slip on the ice. The dad can weigh 1,000 pounds and the mom can way up to 550 pounds. They will walk on the ice and break through the ice and stick their head in the water and come up with their Prey. They like to eat seals. How they hunt for fish is to dive in the water and catch it. Before we go in the closing I want to share something else with you. Did you know Polar Bears are not white but they are clear? The sun reflects on the Polar Bears. I hope you do like learning about Polar Bears.

By: Ryan Burkett
Ms. Sizemore's Class
1st Grade

1.12.15

Snow

Snow is fun but it can be bad when a blizzard forms. It can make it to hard to see. Snow falls as icy crystals. Snow falls mostly in winter when the air is cold.

By: Drew Hurley
Ms. Sizemore's Class
1st Grade
April 21, 2015
Resources:
MyOn, Passage From Jodi Southland

Artic Polar Bears

By Trista Grant

Burr! It's cold here. How do polar bears live in this place? Well we should find out. Let's go! Their Diet. Polar bears mainly eat Ringed Seals and larger seals called, Bearded Seals. They have a lot of blubber so they can get a lot of meat. They are also very common. Polar bears get up eliry so they can sneak into seal's dens. They also eat lots of other animals like Reindeer, Geese, Ducks, and berries. Most of polar bears food is in the water and sometimes they need to get onto an iceberg or land to stay away from their predators.

Where they live Polar bears live in the northern coast of Canada, Greenland, and Russia. They live on the snow. Polar bears sleep more in the day than night because seals are out more at night. Sometimes polar bears lay on their babies to keep them warm at night. Polar bears lay in the middle of snow to nap especially after eating seals. What are their predators. Polar bears predators are sharks and whales. They only swim with their front paws so it's hard for them to swim to shore or an iceberg. Sometimes polar bears fight each other to protect their babies. Their main type of shark that snacks on polar bears is a Great white shark. The main type of whale is a Hump Back

Whale. Well I am going back to study more on polar bears. Catch you later.

Tornado

By Ashley Love

Twister! Twister! Twister! We have to run inside because there is a tornado coming. When there is a tornado coming you should run inside and fine shelter. It can last for a one minute or for an hour. It can damage the earth surface by damaging others houses. The cleanup can last for a long time.

Explain what a tornado is. A tornado is a powerful strong thing that can damage your house. A tornado destroyed whatever it touches. A tornado is really big. You can see a tornado in the clouds. A tornado can be deadly.

How it changes earth surface. It changes the earth surface because it destroy whatever it touches. Also it changes the earth surface because it destroys farms. And it can destroy other schools. Next it can change the earth surface by destroy stores and food. Last it can changes the earth surface by destroys houses.

How they clean up. It takes years to clean up after a tornado. It takes a very long time to build a house or a building. 2,000 people died from deadly tornados. A tornado can cause a lot of damage to the earth surface.

There are 24 deadly `s tornado in the hole world.

I HOPE YOU LEARND A LOT TO DAY ABOUT MY ARTICLE. Did you know that hot air and cold air spins around in a circle to make a tornado. That`s all for today see you later and watch out for those tornados.

Daniel Tharp
September 2015

Dangerous Droughts

Crack! Boom! People get sweaty in a drought. Water is evaporating and the temperature is 115 degrees or more. It is dangerous and they may happen in the spring, summer or fall.

How do they damage the earth? A drought can make a tree break it into fire wood. And it dries earth's ground and plants. The metal on your car is steaming hot! It is like fire on your hand. Now, take a safe place in your house or friend's house and don't go outside.

How hot can it be? Well that was a strong storm. Temperatures can be 130 or more degrees. In a drought, your plants are going to die. In a drought, it will help you to survive and may last a week. Now you know all about a drought and what it does.

Well that was a strong storm you see. Now you know how it starts and end and how it can get.

Polar Bears

Hi my name is Barrett. Polar bears live by eating seals. They eat fish. Polar bears life in the North Pole inside dens. Polar bears dig holes to make caves. They are waiting for seal to come up .They are carnivores and predators. They use there claws to cut their prey. Baby polar bears are called cubs. There is a dad, a mom, a cub. Amazing but true, polar bears fur is clear. I hope you enjoyed learning about a polar bear.

By: Barrett Armstrong
Ms. Sizemore's Class
1st Grade
1.9.15

Lilly Rhoades
October 2014

Tornados!!!

Ooooooo!! What do you know about tornadoes? Well, if you don't, I am going to tell you all about tornadoes. A tornado is limited to a small area, violently destructive windstorm occurring over land. A tornado can do some pretty good damage. It can damage homes, tall buildings, and much more. It can hurt people and maybe kill people too. To stay safe, is to go to a windowless room or basement or you can get hurt or killed, it can break windows, roofs, and walls and more. Wow!! Tornadoes can do lots of damage. It is not really safe to be in something that's not a windowless room or a basement.

Where do tornadoes mostly happen?

Where do tornadoes mostly happen, like literally? Well, if you don't know am telling you! Can you guess where tornados mostly happen? If you got it, great! Now let's see if you got it correct. Well, tornados mostly happen at Tornado Alley. Tornado Alley is in a lot of states and countries. There is a little part that we are in Tornado Alley. The people that live in Tornado Alley is used to tornados. Tornado Alley has a lot of tornadoes. I wonder why Tornado Alley has so many tornadoes. How about you?

<u>How it can kill us! ☹</u> Oh no!! Do you wonder how a tornado can kill us? Well, if you know, great! But if you don't know it's okay because I am going to tell you! A tornado can do a lot of damage so it can kill us or just hurt us. A tornado can blow things up into it. So if it picks you up, you can go to heaven or the sky. It's a little confusing and scarey. But if you don't have a lot of tornadoes where you live your safe as could be.

Wow!! I never want a tornado where I live. Remember to be careful if a tornado is on your way! Now you know what a tornado is, where they mostly happen, and how it can kill us.

Jaden Smith
Mrs.Perry
October 2014

Tsunami Disaster

Crack! Crack! Wash! Danger there is getting ready to be a tsunami that hits Hawaii. You better get to high ground! Did you know a tsunami can wash up beaches and buildings?

Tsunami is Forming A tsunami is a big wave formed by earthquakes or underwater volcanic eruptions!!! Tsunamis are very destructive they can even come up right after earthquakes so be prepared! Tsunamis destroy anything in their ways! GET TO HIGH GROUND!!!!

Stay away A tsunami can wash up land and beaches, so run!!! Tsunamis destroy too much that it may not be able to be repaired.

A tsunami does lots of damage, so if you live beside the ocean, be prepared with money, when a tsunami hits. If you are on the beach and see tsunamis run because it washes up everything! Stay away from a tsunami it will wash you up into the water and drowned you.

Survive it !!!!!!!!!! The only way to survive a tsunami is to get to high ground. Another way to survive a tsunami is to be 1,000 miles away from the beach! To survive a tsunami you have to be 600 feet up in the air.

Tsunamis are really big that's why you have to be really high up. If you want to survive a tsunami, you might want to follow those instructions on how to survive it.

That's all I got about tsunamis and how they change the earth and also how to survive it. That's it for now. Hope I see you again if you survive the tsunami.

9-24-14

Blizzard Warning!

By Marley Long

Woosh! Oh no! It's a blizzard! You might want to take cover when you hear something like this! Blizzards or weather can be very dangerous. You never know it could happen. A blizzard is a long lasting snow storm with intense snow fall. Blizzards make that one spot of the world like an ice cube.

A Blizzard's Brain Blizzards are cold and dark and you never want to get stuck in one. Blizzards are very scary. Blizzards are dangerous too. They're snow storm killing machines with very intense snow fall. They've killed over 1,000 people in the past. They destroy everything in sight. So take cover and stay safe.

Mind Blowing Blizzard Blizzards make you shiver and shake. You can get very hurt or even die if you're outside when a blizzard hits. Blizzards make everything like an ice cube and nothing can stop them. Remember, you don't have another life so you might want to keep living this one! Blizzards freeze rodes and ground. Blizzards change the earth and us because it hurts not just for us, but for the earth. Blizzards can hurt anyone and anything. So keep your pets safe too! Blizzards change everything.

Happy Birthday Blizzard! You never know when a blizzard will come. They always surprise you. They can really scare you! Like a surprise birthday party. Just not a good one! Don't let the blizzard bring you a birthday party! Be careful when it snows too. Because that's where it starts. So **always** be prepared.

As you can see, blizzards are one of mother nature's evil powers aginst us. Everyone needs to be prepared inclouding you so be awear and be prepared! Good by! Thanks for reading!

Scary Storms
by: Kyla Combs in Mrs. Perry`s class

Crack POW boom! Some people scream run and hide when it is raining and lightning strikes. But I am here to tell you a lot of things about tornados. Do you like to learn about different weather than keep on reading? A tornado is a swirling column of air.

Watch out Crash POW! I am going to tell you about tornados some people scream when there is a tornado. A tornado is a violent column of air. It can damage a lot of stuff. For example, a car, a house and a human but if you want you can scream but that's not necessary. Have shelter Hurry theirs a tornado. if you have a shelter than use it. Even for practicing just to be prepared. Damage. A tornado can damage a lot like a car a tree a house and human to.

Earth changing A tornado can change earth by tarring up the ground. And it can last for an hour. It can move faster than 1, 0000 miles per hour.

You may want to practice hiding in your shelter just to make Shure you are safe if it ever happens and trust me it probably will.
Kyla

5-4-15

Alec Britt

Tigers

Tigers eat meat.

Tigers have stripes.

Tigers have big teeth.

5-4-15

Olivia Bryant

Mirror Mirror

Mirror mirror is so tall.

Mirror mirror is so slick.

Mirror mirror falls of the wall.

Mirror mirror breaks.

5-4-15

Jake Jones

Spartans Soccer

I play soccer at the YMCA.

We've won all 8 games we've played.

I'm number 15 and my team is the Spartans.

Every team doesn't want to play us

Because we're so good.

I scored a couple of goals.

5-4-15

Sam Weddle

I Like Dogs

I like dogs.

Dogs are very active.

I have two dogs.

They are named Harvey and Leia.

My dogs are Chihuahuas.

If they fall from too high

They can break their leg.

They can jump very high.

5-4-15

Alex Graham

Red Red Red

Red shoes that roll.

Red socks that glow.

Red shirt that has a soccer ball.

Red box is big.

Red sheet of paper.

5-4-15

Cody Alvey

Dogs

Dogs have sharp claws.

They use the claws in case someone comes.

Dogs are active.

Dogs are big and small.

5-4-15

Cayden Cowan

Dogs

Dogs are cool.

Dogs are cute.

Dogs are fluffy.

Dogs are cool.

Dogs, dogs, dogs.

5-4-15

Aaron Cecil

All About Tigers

Tigers get their stripes from God.

Tigers, tigers

We love tigers.

Tigers go everywhere like us.

5-4-15

Brady Cornell

Baseball

I enjoy baseball because it is fun.

When I get hit and run the bases.

Also it's fun fielding on 1st base

And 2nd base because you get to tag

People with the ball.

5-4-15

Audrey Clarkson

Sewing

I like sewing.

Sewing is fun!

Sewing is interesting!

Sewing is entertaining!

Sewing can fix problems!

5-4-15

Berlyn Jones

Colors

My favorite colors

Are blue, red, and baby blue

These are my favorite colors.

5-4-15

Brayden McMillen

Basketball

Basketball is fun.

I enjoy watching and playing basketball.

Basketball is for all ages.

It is more fun

When I play basketball.

5-4-15

Emma Hallinan

Audrey

I like Audrey because

She is nice to me

And she always solves problems.

5-4-15

Cassidy Ashbaugh

Tigers

I like tigers because

They are orange and cute.

Orange is my favorite color

And tigers are my favorite animal.

5-4-15

Kailey Karner

Colors

There are so many colors

That pink, like light pink

Hot pink and

Violet pink.

5-4-15

Miah Dodd

Summer

On a hot summer day

I like to play.

I love summer.

You get to go swimming.

I play with my dog

And Sydney plays with us.

5-4-15

Trent Woods-Patrick

NBA

Basketball is the best sport.

I like it so much I play it

Every day at home.

NBA has tons of superstars.

You can dunk, you can shoot three's.

5-4-15

Kaden Hendren

Blue

Blue sky

Blue high in the sky

Blue, blue, blue

I can't stop seeing blue.

5-4-15

Wesley Duke

Dogs

Dogs are cool

Dogs are cute

Dogs are fluffy.

Dogs are cool.

Dogs, dogs, dogs.

Emotions

By Emily Haddaway

Are they high, Are the low
Are the fast, are they slow
When you see a cat you want to chase it
When you see a rat you run and hide
One second there one
The next there's none
There like a rover
Emotions all over

Treven's I am poem by: Treven Bentley

I am creative and playful.
I wonder what I'm going to be when I'm odder.
I hear my cats and dogs.
I see the bright blue sky.
I want to be a constructing worker.
I pretend my name is not Treven Bentley.
I fill my soft blanket.
I touch my dog and cat to pet them.
I worry about my family.
I cry when somebody dies in my family.
I am creative and playful.
I understand.
I say thank you to others.
I dream to have mo dreams.
I try to not die.
I hope to not die yet.
I am creative and playful.

I AM POEM by: Cole Cecil

I am generous and funny.
I wonder what other animals live in the sea?
I hear the ocean waves brushing up on shore.
I see becoming a scientist someday.
I want a chemistry laboratory.
I am generous and funny.
I pretend to be a WWE pro wrestler.
I feel good about my future.
I touch a house of jello.
I worry a burglar will rob my house.
I cry when I see somebody die on the news.
I am generous and funny.
I understand fish have to keep swimming to live.
I say kids should make the choices for themselves.
I dream I'm Superman.
I try hard with my schoolwork.
I hope I'm rich as a man.

1-23-15

Dear Ms. Lewis,

I love reading groups because they help me raise my map score.

Reading groups help me on visualizing, schema, visualizing, and inference. Next, reading groups help me on text-to-text, text-to-world, and text-to-self connections.

Reading groups help me to predict, infer, and summarize for my DRA test. I read better now.

This is how reading groups help me learn. I love school so much!

Sincerely,

Madison Baker
Ms. Pinkston's Class, 2nd Grade

2-4-15

Dear Ms. Lewis,

Mr. Vibbert's Compass Lab is the best because he is funny and nice.

Mr. Vibbert is always by my side when I need help. He is there if the computer shuts down.

Mr. Vibbert checks on me when I need to go to the restroom or get drinks from the water fountain.

Mr. Vibbert lets me know when I need to log off and go back to my classroom. I won't be late to leave.

This is why Mr. Vibbert is nice and helps me learn in the Compass Lab.

Sincerely,

Landon Binnix
Ms. Pinkston's Class, 2nd Grade

2-3-15

Dear Ms. Lewis,

You have the best teachers!

All of my teachers push me to do my best. Also, my teachers are nice, kind, and polite and never mean to me. They never yell at me. That is why your teachers are nice.

My teachers give me fun lessons. I also get challenging lessons, too! They help me learn a lot. Ms. Miller makes fun reading lessons. Ms. Cooper also makes fun math lessons for me and Ms. Pinkston.

My teachers have fire drills to keep us safe, in case we have a fire. I always feel safe at school because we do drills.

Your teachers make learning fun!

Sincerely,

Liam Chism
Ms. Pinkston's Class, 2nd Grade

1-23-15

Dear Ms. Lewis,

Thank you for giving me great reading time because it is super fun! Reading is fun because I find interesting details in my texts. It is also fun because I can read in reading groups.

I really, really, really love my quiet, deep-reading time because on one is bothering me. I love my quiet reading time, also, because I can read alone.

I read happily because I am always on my best. I also am very good at chunking words.

Thank you for the reading program at MWES. It is very, very, fun! Thank you.

Sincerely,

Jonah Clements-Mattingly
Ms. Pinkston's Class, 2nd Grade

2-4-15

Dear Ms. Lewis,

I love to learn in Mr. Kerr's Music class.

In Music, we get to sing the "Now" songs. We learn to sing them and we are good at it.

I love Music because we get to sing "Now" songs and funny songs. I love music because I get to sing a lot of different songs.

Mr. Kerr teaches us cool songs, fun songs, and nice songs. He lets me have a partner to sing with.

Mr. Kerr lets us watch music videos that show us how to sing. Watching music videos helps me sing better.

This is why I love school and music at MWES!

Sincerely,

Gracie Dockery
Ms. Pinkston's Class, 2nd Grade

1-23-15

Dear Ms. Lewis

I love you to the moon and back thank you for hiring Ms. Pinkston.

Ms. Pinkston gives me lots of HOTQs (Higher Order Thinking Questions). HOTQs make me think harder.

Word Works helps me be a good reader. I am learning to chunk words better.

Reading makes my MAP scores go higher. We read every day.

Sincerely,

Jay Duncan
Ms. Pinkston's Class, 2nd Grade

1-23-15

Dear Ms. Lewis,

I'd like to thank you for the wonderful way you lead our school.

I really love my teachers, and I love working with them. First, I love my teachers because they have the best lessons ever and they make learning fun.

Second, I love Ms. Pinkston, Ms. Miller, and Ms. Grau because they are the best loving and caring teachers a student could have. They make me love reading and math and want to do harder problems.

Third, I love my teachers because they love me and always help me when I am stuck. They help me and then push me to always do better and harder work.

So, this is why I love my teachers.

Sincerely,

Kyle Fryrear
Ms. Pinkston's Class, 2nd Grade

2-3-15

Dear Ms. Lewis,

I love science at MWES.

I love science because it tells you what is in life. My favorite lesson that Ms. Young taught is Sink-and-Float.

The Sink-and-Float was a game where we put in objects and estimated if the objects would sink or float. Some of the objects were heavy and some were light. A lot of the objects sank.

I learned a lot about what makes things float or sink. The Sink-and-Float game was fun.

This is just one reason why I love science at MWES.

Love,

Lizzy Hallinan
Ms. Pinkston's Class, 2nd Grade

1-23-15

Dear Ms. Lewis,

You are the best principal a school could ever have. You lead great Pow-Wows!

I just wanted to say that I love the awards like the Writing Wall of Fame. I also love math, art, language arts, and science.

The Pow-Wows at this school are great. Our Pow-Wows are always fun and make me feel happy to be part of MWES.

The thing I like most at the Pow-Wows is you! No matter if I get an award or not, you are always there to support me.

These are the reasons why MWES has the best Pow-Wows.

Sincerely,

Addyson Hatter
Ms. Pinkston's Class, 2nd Grade

2-4-15

Dear Ms. Lewis,

I am writing to you because I want to tell you what helps me learn at MWES. Learning is fun with a principal like you!

Reading and writing help me learn all the time. I am learning how to read and write a letter with paragraphs.

I also wanted to tell you that checking out books in Ms. Hutchins's library helps me read. The library helps me because I can get "Just-Right" books.

Ms. Pinkston helps me learn. She pushes me to read higher books. I am reading Junie B. Jones, now, and it is getting easier to read. The "Focus "Button" helps me learn because I pay attention and really listen.

I love being a Peer Tutor in reading. It is fun to help my friends with their reading. Being a Peer Tutor makes me a leader in my class.Now you know what helps me learn at MWES!

Sincerely,

Brook-Lynn Helm
Ms. Pinkston's Class, 2nd Grade

2-4-15

Dear Ms. Lewis,

You pick the best Marvelous Monday people. They bring in rally cool animals.

I like the plays. I love watching the actors. They are awesome.

I like Marvelous Mondays because each time we hear new speakers. They talk about how to care about others.

You are the best principal in the world.

Sincerely,

Nick Huff
Ms. Pinkston's Class, 2nd Grade

2-3-15

Dear Ms. Lewis,

I love to read in reading groups. It makes me happy.

I love to read and write about my book. I try to read better every day. I love to read so much.

I work hard to read and write. I love to read every time. I get to read for 20 minutes. I love to read every day. I try to read carefully. I try to push the class to read better.

I love to read in reading workshop. I work hard to be the best reader.

Sincerely,

Brady Israel
Ms. Pinkston's Class, 2nd Grade

1-23-15

Dear Ms. Lewis,

The Special Area teachers (Coach Belk, Mr. Kerr, Ms. Hutchins, and Ms. Young) let us have fun with learning. They show me videos so I can visualize higher learning.

The Special Area teachers let me learn by using my senses like listening, visualizing, and smelling. My senses help me understand higher texts.

The Special Area teachers help me with my humungous problems. I am learning to solve my own problems because they teach us problem-solving.

This is why the Special Area teachers are nice.

Sincerely,

Bailey Karner
Ms. Pinkston's Class, 2nd Grade

2-4-15

Dear Ms. Lewis,

I like to study science at MWES. Science is fun to learn.

I love to study food chains. The sun feeds the plants. The plants feed the animals. The animals feed other animals.

In Ms. Young's Stem Lab, I learned to do scientific experiments. We tested the water to make it clean.

I like to study fossils. Ms. Young showed us a fossil of a sea creature. Fossils tell us which plants and animals lived a long time ago.

These are the reasons I like to study science at MWES. Ms. Lewis is the best principal ever!

Sincerely,

Christian Maurer
Ms. Pinkston's Class, 2nd Grade

2-3-15

Dear Ms. Lewis,

I love math because it is fun to learn. Mc. Cooper makes lesson plans that are fun for 2nd grade.

My favorite math is measurement. I like using a ruler and yard stick. We measure inches, centimeters, and feet.

Math makes me happy, like when I'm on the playground. I love multiplication because it's really hard and I love to do hard things.

Subtraction is cool because you regroup. Regrouping is hard. I'm still practicing regrouping.

Math is important to me because, when you buy shoes or something else you need, Ms. Pinkston says you need to know math to live.

Sincerely,

Abbie McCoy
Ms. Pinkston's Class, 2nd Grade

1-30-15

Dear Ms. Lewis,

I like when Ms. Franklin comes into our classroom because she teaches us new counseling lessons.

Ms. Franklin teaches us the word of the week. The word of the week can make others feel good, like the word, "kindness."

I like when Ms. Franklin reads us interesting books. She read a book about "Tattle Tongue." I learned you don't have to always tattle on somebody. Sometimes, you can make an "I" statement.

Ms. Franklin taught us about not bullying. She says that we should be nice to each other and never say mean things to others.

This is why I love Ms. Franklin.

Sincerely,

Lily Merkle
Ms. Pinkston's Class, 2nd Grade

2-3-15

Dear Ms. Lewis,

Thank you for making this school because this school is cool, fun, and I love learning. Ms. Pinkston helps me because she helps with hard, misspelled words. She also helps me with math and writing.

Ms. Pinkston helps us a lot and pushes the class to think harder and learn new things. Then, I push myself to learn. I remember when I learned to visualize. Ms. Pinkston had me close my eyes and visualize parts of a story. Visualizing really helps me when I am reading *Lemony Snickets*. *Lemony Snickets* is a good book to read. I want to read all 13 books in the series.

I love it when we play learning games. They are so much fun and cool. We played a dice game where we were in groups. We used place value to find the biggest number after we rolled the dice. It was so fun. Ms. Pinkston really helps the class a lot, and she is very funny, too. She makes learning fun.

Your friend,

Madisyn Skaggs
Ms. Pinkston's Class, 2nd Grade

2-4-15

Dear Ms. Lewis,

I love this school because you hire nice Lunchroom Ladies!

I love this school because the Lunch Ladies have a smile on their faces every day. They are very friendly.

Ms. Lyn and Ms. Starla help me open my silverware packet. They take the time to come and check on us to see if we need anything.

When I say, "Thank you," the lunch ladies always say, "You're welcome."

Mt. Washington Elementary School has the best food in the world!

Sincerely,

Danika Street
Ms. Pinkston's Class, 2nd Grade

1-30-15

Dear Ms. Lewis,

I'm happy that you are in school so that I can tell you about science.

Science gives me more schema. I have new schema on animals from Ms. Young.

I use my thinking strategies in science lab. I love visualizing about solids, liquids, and gasses.

I once was in science and I was making connections. I connected to a carnivore. It was a bear. Bears eat meat and fruit, which I like.

I hope my letter makes your schema grow!

Love,

Jacob Walls
Ms. Pinkston's Cass, 2nd Grade

1-30-15

Dear Ms. Lewis,

Thank you for having us do Math Automaticity. I have the most fun ever.

Automaticity helps me so much that I raised my Math MAP score very high. Automaticity always helps me.

Sometimes, I can't wait for Math Automaticity. Math makes me so excited!!!

Math Automaticity helps me learn multiplication better. If I work hard enough, I can learn division.

This is why I love Math Automaticity.

Sincerely,

Matthew Wheeler
Ms. Pinkston's Class, 2nd Grade

1-30-15

Dear Ms. Lewis,

Thank you for MAP testing. It helps me a lot.

I love MAP testing because Ms. Pinkston helps us with goal setting. I can see how great I am learning in class.

Ms. Pinkston gives me lots of HOTQs (Higher Order Thinking Questions). Also, HOTQs make me think harder for the MAP test.

Reading groups and math groups help me on MAP tests. Reading groups help because Peer Tutors help me chunk new words. Math groups give me problems to solve.

Again, thank you for everything you've done to help me learn.

Sincerely,

Maya Willis
Ms. Pinkston's Class, 2nd Grade

Jaylen Wheatley
2nd Grade
Mrs. Cooper

Legend: How a Camel got Its Humps

Three years ago, when the world was new, a camel was really lazy and was sitting down all day. When he bullied an animal he would get a hump. A zebra asked him "do you want to play"? He said "no you are weird". Then he got a hump. Then the zebra left and the camel relaxed some more. Then a pig came over and said "Oink Oink"! Do you want to play"? The camel said "why would I play with you"? And the pig said "excuse me". So then a horse came and said "Do you want to play?" He said "don't ask me that again and I mean it!!!" So then camel kept on bullying other animals and grew more and more humps every day.

Lily Ralston
2nd Grade
Mrs. Cooper

Fable: Milly the Monkey

Once upon a time there was a monkey named Milly and she was sometimes good and sometimes bad. But one day she was bad. Well it all started when she was at school coloring. Her friend grabbed the last marker and Milly grabbed the last marker too. Then Milly grabbed it from her friend and they got in a fight. Then her teacher saw. They had a talk. The teacher asked “who had it first?” Milly said “I did.” But Milly`s teacher just knew that Milly did not. Milly`s teacher said “Milly you did not” then Milly sighed and gave the marker back. But Milly still got in trouble for lying .The moral of the story is to always tell the truth.

Be Nice to One of Other's
by Emma Brogan

I might be deferent but I steel fit in......

One's a pond of time there was a boy named Jacky and he lived in Mt.Washingten Kentucky. And he loved the song Shake it off by Taylor Swift, And Jacky Dances to it all day long but he's not like other people in his grade because Jacky has this disease called Down syndrome.

Down syndrome is one his brain does not learn how old he is .That means he talks deferent looks deferent then other people. Next morning his mom named Christy woke them up. Christy is 39 years old and she has blackish brownish hair. Also brown eyes and she's 5 foot 2 .and she's coo co crazy insane about u of L. She likes them because her whole family likes U of L too.

And Jacky has a little brother named brody and he loves u of L to, well some times because he's a follower not a leader that's what his mom says .brody has brown eyes and brown Carly heir.

The boys woke up and ate some breakfast and Jacky had chocolate pop tarts and to drink he had orange juice. And Brody had captain crunch cereal with milk and Christy also had captain crunch cereal with milk. All of them got ready but Christy had to get Jacky's shoes on and tie them for school. Then Christy had to get Brody's jeans on for school.

Jacky had a red stripe shirt on and navy brown short. Brody had on a blue underwater shark shirt on and jeans on. Christy had on a black t shirt on and a red scarf and jeans on with diamonds on the said but they are fake. Then Christy had to take brody to school he's in first grade and he goes to crossroads elementary school and he plays for their flag football team and he the hiker or the sinter.

And then Christy had to take Jacky to he's school. And it wear kids like him go to this special school wear people with any dizzies and to get better treatment and more care. Also Jacky has 3 best friend's Becky, Josh, and Isabell. Josh and Becky have Down syndrome and Isabell has cerebral palsy. Cerebral palsy is won you cannot talk at all so she has a bored that has words on it to point at the words.

Then it was lunch time. Jacky had a peace of pizza with chees. Then it was time to go home .Jacky is a car raider and Becky is a walker also josh is a walker and Isabell is a bus rider.

When Jacky got home his nana was there setting on the couch. Then Jacky thought in his head she must have got out of work early. But she had a silly look on her face so something is going on.

Then nana said "you are going to move to a deferent school a real high school"

Then Jacky said "wear is mom and way I am I moving?

"Because you and mom and brody have to move to a deferent house side nana"ok wear is mom "At your new school checking you in' 'said nana "well ok" said Jacky.

Next morning Jacky was at his knew school Don don don!!!!!!! Jacky is now in hid knew school it is called east side middle school and then Jacky walked in to his knew school and he saw no body at all so he got confused and then he saw a class room and so he walked in and kids wear staring at him and then he walked to his desk and then everybody was laughing and pointing at him then then teacher said "one more peep you are going to the principal offices and something bad well happen. Then he was sad and then he left the room in sadness.

Then the teacher was rushing with him and yelled," Jacky come back into this class room right this instant!" then the teacher gave up. But this big, mean bully in the class room didn't give up. And then he chased him into the bathroom. And said,"You are not like other kids in the class. You are different than other kids."

Then Jacky rushed to the principal's office. He tried to say," I want to go home." Then the principle said, "Why do you want to go home?" "This big mean bully name Nicky said I was deferent and know I want to go home said Jacky then the principal said ok I well take you home but know you have to stand up to him and say stop what you are doing it's mean to do that to a person. Well ok I well do that said Jacky. Then Jacky's mom came and said "why do you want leave your new school? 'Because this big mean bully said something mean to me and know I am scared of him "why are you scared of him said Christy?" because he said you are not like other kids in class room, and you are deferent" and so then I told the principal to tell you that I want to go home and never come back said Jacky well you only have to go to school tomorrow and tell that bully to stop what you are doing to me and what you are doing to everybody eels in the school and out of school" said Christy.

Next morning Jacky was ready to tell that bully to stop!! Stop!! Stop!! Stop what you are doing it is mean to do that to me and everybody eels and say sorry. Jacky was motivated to tell that mean bully. Then Christy said, “It is time to go.” Then Jacky said, “I will meet you in the car.” Then Brody and Jacky were heading to their school. When Jacky went onto the school doors, out of the corner of his eye he saw Nicky the bully, he was by the lockers and he was standing there all tough. Then Jacky walked over there and said to him,

“I don’t like you doing this to me and everyone else so you need to stop it because it is mean and know I am going to move schools all because of you’’ then the bully side ‘’I know I am very sorry and you do not have to move’ ’then Jacky said ’’ but you are bully and you should not say nice things at all you are a bully!!!!!! Then Nicky said’’ well I could say bad things about you but I am choosing to say nice things to you. Can we please be friends at least’’ Said Nicky ‘ well ok but you have to be nice to me for now on’’ said Jacky ‘’I swear I changed’’ said Nicky ‘’why did you changed’’ said Jacky’’ the principal said something to me and so I changed’’ said Nicky ’’ well ok said Jacky, and they were best friends but Jacky is all way’s normal and he knows it no matter what people say to him!!!

Aubrey Ernst
2nd Grade
Mrs. Cooper

Legend: How Your Thumb Got on the Other Side of Your Hand

Once upon a time long long ago there were four fingers named Bob, Jerald, Rocky, and Jim. They were mean, rude, and angry. Then there was a thumb named Tom. He was all lonely, and he was caring, loving, and also sad.

One day Bob, Jerald, Rocky, and Jim got into a big fight. So then they said "there's no reason to be fighting so let's just pick on Tom the thumb". So everyone said yes or ok. So they did. Some of the things they said where you stink and you look ugly. Then the day after that happened the thumb decided to move away from Bob, Jerald, Rocky, and Jim the four fingers. Ever since the thumb moved away from the four fingers, he has not liked them. He hasn't moved back since.

Blue Sky

By Chloe Sherlock

Chapter 1 Getting a Horse

My name is Skylier Moon Realiy. I'm 9 years old. I have an older sister that's 14 her name is Rachel. You can call me Sky. I live with pigs, cows, sheep, goats, dogs, cats, rabbits, chickens, and ducks but no horses! For my 10th birthday my papa buyed me a horse. I screamed in joy. YAY! YAY! YAY! My papa said know you hafe to take care of it. I said I promise I will. He asked what are you going to name her? I yelled Ginger! He said ok lets go get her trailer and stuff. I yelled YAY! She had black hair and brown fur. I love living at my grandma and grandpas farm. I love all the animals. I hafe to do choirs and it's a whole olt of work taking care of animals!

Chapter 2 Training Time

The next day I woke up I was very exited cause it was the first day of training! I had to teach ginger. I wanted to walk her with a lead rope. But every time I tried ginger wanted to go off and lollygag in they other direction. Ahhh! I wanted to teach her to eat oats from my hand so I had to bribe her with an apple. I love ginger very much she is buitiful but she is a STUBERN HORSE!!! I hafe to brush her every day to keep her fur shiny.

Chapter 3 Trying to Ride

After feeding the animals my grandpa came outside and tried to help me ride. But ginger ran off every time.

Chapter 4 The Injury

When grandpa was trying to teach me how to ride a horse. Ginger got scared and kicked me in the arm and leg. I got a big bruise on my leg that would make me cry every time something tuched it. My arm broke. I wore a blue cast.

Chapter 5 Staying in Bed

I hafe to stay in bed until my injury is better. My choirs are are held back. So my grandma has to do them.

Chapter 6 Healed

2 months later my arm and leg was healed. And I went outside to play cause I was real

exsited. So I grabbed my hat and thought it's ridding time!

Chapter 7 Learning How

I was walking my other horse cole. He was black so was his hair when I seen a mare white and so was her hair. I pulled out my lasso and wosh! I caught her me and cole pulled her all the way home. When my grandma saw her she said, "Skylier were did you get that mare? Bring her to your barn house not your traylier. She laid down and went to sleep with cole I locked my barn. And went to the traylier and went to sleep.

Chapter 8 Babys

The next day I went to the barn house and the mare had fowles. I named the mare snow but cole choosed it he pointed his nose at a picture in the barn with snow. Snow had 3 fowls. We named the 3rd fowl lilly.

Chapter 9 Ridding Ginger

I got on ginger when my papa said don't be scared know I said I'm not. Then I mad sure I was comfterable then I took off I had to hang on very tight!

Chapter 10 OH! NO!

I went to the hospital because my mom was having another baby. I don't want a little brother or sister! Uhhh! Now I'll hafe to watch him or her all the time. 5 hours later...My mom screamed, pouted, yelled and most of all cryed because she was hurting bad then the doctor put numming medicine on her so it wouldn't hurt. As soon as the docter said there was going to be a boy I cheered then he said his coculations were wrong it's a girl. I was roaring mad! My mom said hey Skylier why don't you name her I said boo. I thought and thought and the first name I came up with was cloudy. Mom said that's her nickname. Natilie? I said middle said mom Emily! She said perfect. I said goody me mom said don't be like that you got a sister you should be thankful!

About characters:

Skylier = Jessie my older sister that's 13
Rachel = my older sister Kayla that's 24
Grandma = my grandma
Grandpa = my grandpa
Mom = my mom
Emily = me

When Pigs Fly

One day there was a pig named Jeffrey. He worked at the piggy experiment station. Jeffrey was going to be to be the first pig to fly to the MOON!

When it was time to launch Jeffrey was exited. He was thinking about how great it would be as the first pig on that big sphere of night light. 10, 9,8,7,6,5,4,3,2,1, Blast-Off! The rocket blazed quickly into the clouds. The ride was very bumpy. Now Jeffrey was nervous not exited. Just a he began to feel calm again, his rocket exploded and Jeffrey went flying!

But the most unlikely thing happened... Jeffrey grew wings!

Jeffrey was not the first pig to fly to the moon, but he was the first pig to grow wings!

THE END

Written by Evan Hall
Third Grade
Mrs. Dixon

Sucked In

By Jared St. Clair

"Whirl" Mikes Xbox sounded.

"Ah I'm getting sucked in" said Mike.

Three hours earlier Mike and his friend Will were playing Xbox. Mike has brown hair and green eyes. When they got done they went to turn it off and it sucked them in.

"To get out we need to get to the central control panel" said Mike.

"Ok" said Will.

They headed toward the first game they had to complete. "We need to compete the Minecraft tutorial" said will.

When they spawned they were in an arena death match. Each of them had swords and armor. Both of them lived and moved on to madden NFL 15 and were losing 6 to 15. They needed at least 2 touchdowns to win. "Here comes Will down the field to get a touchdown" says reporter Brown.

"The Patriots hold the ball now, oh and an interception by the Seahawks. With seven seconds left will mike be able to score the winning touchdown." Says reporter Brown.

"Mike did it." Said Will.

They warped out of the game and were close to the central control panel. They got there and flipped the switches and started messing with wires. Will cut the wrong wire and made a fire, fortunately right that second they got out of it. They picked it up and put it in the yard sale. It got sold and everything was fine. “That was scary” said Mike.

“Yeah” said Will.

Pinkie and Gumball Away

By: The magical Cierra Hermann

One fine morning Pinkie and gumball were at an ice cream shop when suddenly they heard a strange noise coming from outside of the shop. Well of course we know that Pinkie and Gumball always go to check it out. The noise was coming from a dark ally. When they got to the ally the strange noise stopped. "That's so weird, it's like it saw us coming or something like that." When they got back to the ice cream shop the sneaky noise started again. This time they were smart so they looked through the window. This time they saw a…you don't want to know…okay if you insist…you know I really can't do this…"Get on with it!" Pinkie let me calm down first! They saw a UFO! Yes I said that they saw a UFO! Okay now back to the story. So the two uni… "Hey we still haven't introduced ourselves yet!" Fine do your thing! "Hello everybody I'm Pinkie the unicorn and this is my friend Super Gumball, she's a unicorn as well. Hello it's so nice to meet you all and as Pinkie said I am the magical Super Gumball and I am here to shine!" Gumball didn't your mommy tell you not to brag! Okay where was I, oh yes they saw a UFO!

Pinkie had just recently gotten all the super powers in the world in the story The Volcano Surprise so she turned herself and Gumball invisible. They ever so slowly walked toward the strange ship. The invisibility had worn of and the UFO vanished. They knew it was there so they simply touched it and everything went blank. The two heroes went into a deep sleep and started to float away with the UFO. When they woke up they forgot all about what had just happened. "Where are we?" Asked Gumball confused. "You are in a highly unidentified flying object. Also known as a HUFO". Said the two aliens. "AHHHHHHHHH!!!!! STRANGER DANGER! STRANGER DANGER!" Screamed pinkie. "We are not strangers we are Balloon and Crayola". "Here let us show you around a little bit".
After Balloon and Crayola showed them around Pinkie suggested that they should get going. "No you can't go you must stay here forever"!!! "What do you mean forever"? "I mean that you have to stay here FOREVER"!!!!!! That's crazy isn`t it! I mean I didn't think our super heroes would die like this. Seriously did you think they would die like this?! You know their the amazing Pinkie the Unicorn and Super Gumball!!! Did you know they fought Purplie the evil unicorn! Sorry about that, now back to the story.so, Crayola and Balloon took them to their room

and locked them in. “Gumball we have to do something about this!” Or we could do nothing about it and just relax forever.” ‘How about we take a nerf gun and shoot the walls until they fall down!”

“Pinkie you know we could just crawl through this window.” Ha, do you want to know something that I should have told Pinkie a long time ago? They’re in outer space so they can`t breathe out there. Isn’t that so funny? Wait if they can’t if they can’t breathe then their story can’t go on and the worst thing is… I won’t get paid! WAIT! Don’t go out the window, I can just erase one of the walls! “Fine, but do it quietly.” Pinkie you’re so mean! Here we go. “Wait!” What is it Pinkie? “I want to sing an inspirational song, it’s called Onions.” “Onions, onions, onions.” “Thank you!” “Wait just a second, why should we listen to you?” “Come on Pinkie let’s go!” No wait! I love yo… but it was too late for me to finish my own sentence! When Pinkie and Gumball woke up they were in the hospital. “What happened to us?” Asked Gumball in a confused voice. “You fell of a roof and Pinkie fell from the sky and hit a trash can.” “Oh that’s really harsh!” So let’s go from lamesville and go to Broadway!!! ☺☺☺☺☺☺☺☺☺☺☺ Pinkie and Gumball wondered if the UFO thing was all a very bad dream. “BEEP BOOP BOP!” “Is that you Balloon?” “Yes and don’t forget about Crayola. We need you back on the

UFO!!!" ☹ "Why?" Bob and Hair have died and we need to go to the past to get them back!!!" "Wow, so much happens when you fall from the sky and hit a trash can." Pinkie is so weird isn't she? "No I'm not… I just have problems. So Pinkie, Gumball, Balloon, and Crayola went to the UFO to go get Bob and Hair back. What they were soon to find out was that this was all a…hold on a second. Pause the story! PAUSE. It was all a big joke! You'll learn more about the joke later on in the story. Now you can play the story! PLAY. So the all got in the space ship and typed the word past in the search pad. "Wait we are in a UFO not a space ship." Oh I forgot. I wish Pinkie couldn't hear me! "I heard that!" So they zoomed to the past to bring back Bob and Hair. They went so fast that Crayola and Balloon flew back hit the wall. Seconds later they slowly melted and Bob and Hair appeared. "What are you two doing here?" Yelled Gumball angrily. Were… so, so, so sorry this was all a big joke!" Said hair dramatically. "Yeah, we promise that it won't happen again!" "Bob." "Yes Pinkie?" "I'm waiting." "Fine, we Pinkie promise." Hey stick to the program! "You better watch your back Mrs. Narrator!" My name is Narrator Narrator! Now back to the story. "Can you ever forgive us?" "No, but we can make you dance in kitten costumes!" ☺☺☺ "But I'm allergic to cats!" said Hair. "Deal with it!" So I guess this is the end of our tale. "Yes it is Narrator

Narrator." Hey you remembered my name! ☺☺ "Yes, because you're my friend." Oh Pinkie I love you so much! "Wait it's not the end, here come the credits!

Credits

Yes this is the credits. I was only doing this for the dough. If you were my friend you would know that I love cookies. This isn't in the script but I love to get of topic! Credits, I don't like my job but I still do it for the dough. So that was cool. Wait that doesn't make any sense at all. So…well…um… yeah. This is the end of the credits so…bye!

☺☺Goodbye!!!

Fluffy Unicorn Land

By: Ella Deweese

*2015 District Young Authors Finalist, 4th Grade

One day I walked outside after an amazing breakfast of waffles and toast, to find a shovel on the back porch. The shovel had a note on it that said" dig under the oak tree." So I started digging.

When I started digging deep in the ground my shovel hit something metal. It was a metal box! The box had the words "Fluffy unicorn land "engraved on the front.

I opened the box, and inside was a portal! The portal pulled me in instantly! It took me to a land of unicorns, candy and clouds that barfed rainbows. When I stepped out of the portal I saw a unicorn, so I walked up and asked him "where am I?" so the unicorn said "You are in Fluffy unicorn Land!"

So I started walking around because I really wanted to see what Fluffy Unicorn land looks like. This land is way different than where I'm from, this place has walking waffles and clouds barfing rainbows.

As I walked around I started noticing life size candy all around me but when I saw the life size Twix candy bar I just attacked it. Because looked so (B.T.W Twix is my favorite candy bar ever!) When I was walking I saw a walking waffle and I asked him "How long do I have to stay here?" And he said "As long as you want."

It was very hard choosing if I wanted to stay or leave. After about two hours of thinking I decided to stay one day an see if I
Like it.

So after eating that life size Twix Bar I needed to wash up. I started walking around to try and find water. After a long time of walking I finely found water. But when I put the water on my face my face turned RAINBOW! Then out of know where
Hello kitty was running down the street saying "The evil is coming!" and I said "What evil?" but she just said "No time just go." So I started running, so fast that I ran rite back into the portal.

So I lived happily ever after (still with a rainbow face!)

Upcoming Star

Once, there was a Yorkshire terrier named Crystal 2 months old, who loved to shop. She had an owner named Joy Anna. Joy Anna was a superstar at 18.

She took good care of Crystal "woof." "Be quite Crystal!" Joy Anna commanded! As you Know Joy Anna is a Superstar so Crystal has to be a royal dog. She even takes her out, feeds her and much more. She even takes her on Road trips. That's crazy.

One day Crystal was about to go on a road trip with Joy Anna. They were going to Hollywood! Joy Anna woke Crystal up. Joy Anna told Crystal that we are going to go to Hollywood! Crystal barked with delight! Calm Down Crystal! Do you know what's insane? Crazy Crystal has her own suitcase! I mean her own suitcase? Her own outfits? I mean I don't even have my own suitcase! That's radical! So Lexie and Crystal started packing their bags, well of course Crystal can't pack her own bag because she doesn't have hands so Lexie packed Crystal's bag.

Finally, it was time to leave to go to Hollywood so they got packed up and got in the car. Crystal had her own seat in the front. She is so spoiled. So the 4 hour drive was over and they got there and they had their own house to stay in. Crystal ran in the house. "woof!" I have a feeling that Joy Anna won't be the only superstar in the family!

Written by Adyson Mudd
3rd Grade
Mrs. Dixon

Pistol and the Portal Trouble:

By Lucas Taylor

Once there was a dog by the name of Pistol Pete. Some people called him Pistol. Pistol loved chewing rawhide bones with bacon essence.

One day, his bone came to life. The bone said, "I was sprinkled by fairy dust."

Follow me I will take you to a magical place called Bone Land.

The dog asked, "How?"

"Through a magic tree portal," said the bone.

He got to Bone Land safe. Suddenly he got super ninja powers from a wizard. Then he fought all the evil bones because they wanted him gone.

Then he was lost in the 3rd galaxy. It was called the 2045 Galaxy. It was covered in purple spikes that didn't hurt.

"How do I get out of here?" said Pistol.

"Pistol, we have to use a portal," said the not so evil bone.

"I'm lost without my owner," Pistol said.

"You'll be home soon."

"And we need to build the new portal to get back home," said Pistol.

"What do you mean us? I'm the one who brought you," said the bone.

Suddenly they heard an evil laugh. It was an evil bone.

"How are they evil anyway?" asked Pistol.

"An evil wizard got them."

Just then, Pistol said I found the portal. It was camouflaged in this wall.

"Jump in quick!" exclaimed the bone. "I told you we would find it." After that, Pistol and the bone lived happily ever after.

The Two Kingdoms

by Jude Russelburg

*2015 District Young Authors Runner-Up, 2nd Grade

I dedicate this book to my brother Brayden because he encourages me to be brave and even get into a boucy house.

Once there were two kingdoms. There was a good kingdom in a land far away on the hills and it had straight dangling vines on it. The vines had pretty pink and purple flowers on it. The castle was tall and had gray stones on it and it was on a hill. It was as tall as a skyscraper.

In the dark forest far away the evil kingdom was on a mountain far in the woods and there was a witch who lived in the top room. It was hard to climb because there were sharp sticks and rocks.

One day the evil king came in to the good kings palace and shouted with a voice like death "There will be a war! " The villagers were scared and they coward and ran into their houses.

It happened the next day when the evil king crashed into the glass windows with fire balls. They were as big as boulders. The king tried to call his army but he couldn't because the evil king already called his army to the village.

The witch appeared with potions on her belt. She pulled out two potions. The blue one was lightning and the red was fire. She poured them in the cauldron together and she put her wand in there and she waved the wand around and put a spell right in the middle of the army and blew them far far apart.

The good King got his soul took away when the village was destroyed. The king became boney and his skin soaked up with his bones. He fell to the ground and at that moment everything changed. All that remained was broken gray stones and dust.

Deep under the destruction there were the pink flowers of hope. They grew a new village slowly. A flower queen emerged. This made that evil king angry.

The strength of the flowers made a force field of hope and it could never be destroyed. The evil king retreat in and his castle forever.

NOW AVAILABLE!!!

Poop Happens!" in this send up of all things cowboy!

So, Who Was That Masked Guy Anyway? is the story of Ernie, the grandson of the original Masked Cowboy, a lawman who fought for truth, justice and the cowboy way in the old west. Now that Grandpa is getting on in years he's looking for someone to carry on for him. The only problem? Ernie doesn't know anything about being a cowboy. He's never seen a real cow, he's allergic to milk and to tell the truth he doesn't know one end of a horse from another! So it's off to cowboy school to learn the basics of cowboyology. He'll learn to rope and ride, chew and spit and to develop the perfect "Yee-Haw!". And it's a good thing, because a band of no good outlaws have captured the good people of Gabby Gulch and the President of the United States, Theodore Roosevelt! Now it's up to Ernie and his friends to save the day...but beware, before it's all over, the poop is sure to hit the fans!

NOW AVAILABLE!!!

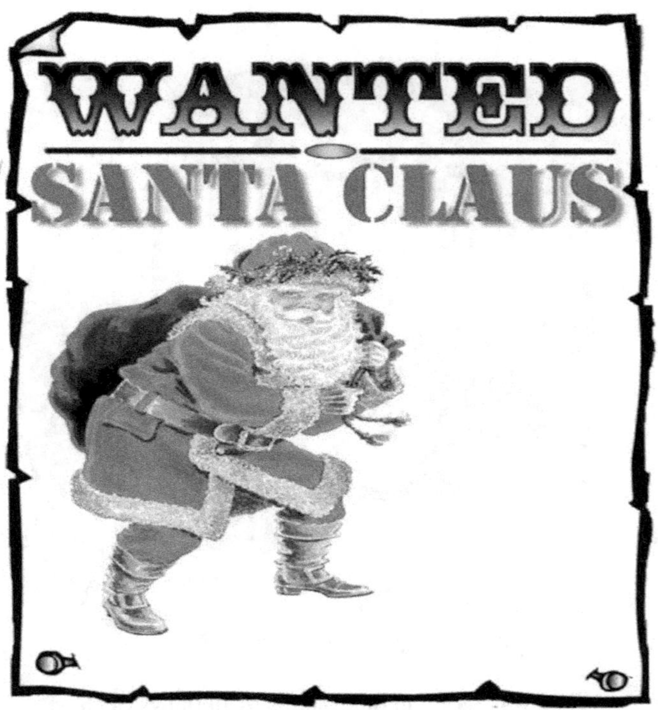

WANTED: SANTA CLAUS is the story of what happens when a group of department store moguls led by the greedy B. G. Bucks decide to replace Santa Claus with the shiny new "KRINGLE 3000", codenamed...ROBO-SANTA! A new Father Christmas with a titanium alloy outer shell housing a nuclear powered drive train, not to mention a snow white beard and a jolly disposition! These greedy tycoons will stop at nothing to get rid of jolly old St. Nick. That includes framing him for such crimes as purse snatching, tire theft and...oh no...not.....puppy kicking??!! Say it isn't so Santa! Now it's up to Santa's elves to save the day! But Santa's in no shape to take on his stainless steel counterpart! He'll have to train for his big comeback. Enter Mickey, one of the toughest elves of all time! He'll get Santa ready for the big showdown! But it's going to mean reaching deep down inside to find "the eye of the reindeer"!

NOW AVAILABLE!!!

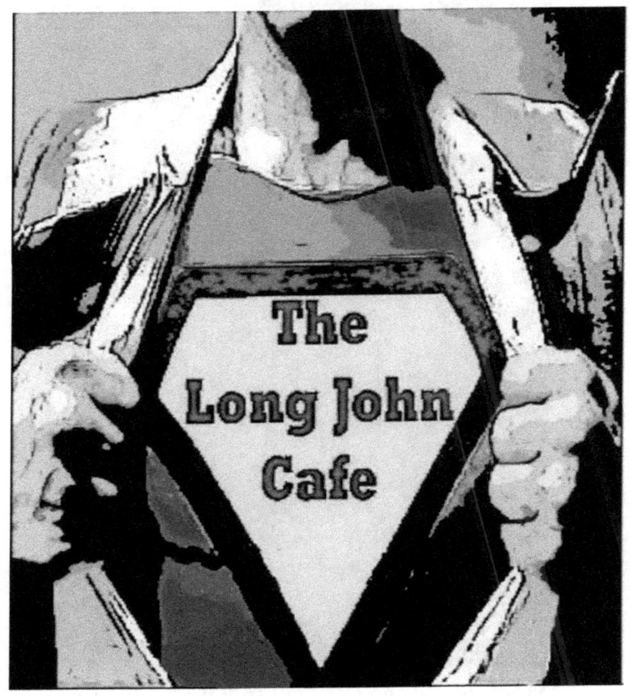

At the edge of the universe sits The Long John Cafe. A place where the average guy and the average "Super" guy can sit and have a cup of coffee and just be themselves...or, someone else if that's what they want. The cafe is populated by iconic figures of the 20th Century, including cowboys, hippies, super heroes and movie stars. They've come to celebrate the end of the old Century and the beginning of tomorrow! That is, if they make it through the night! It seems the evil Dr. McNastiman has other plans for our heroes. Like their total destruction!

NOW AVAILABLE!!!

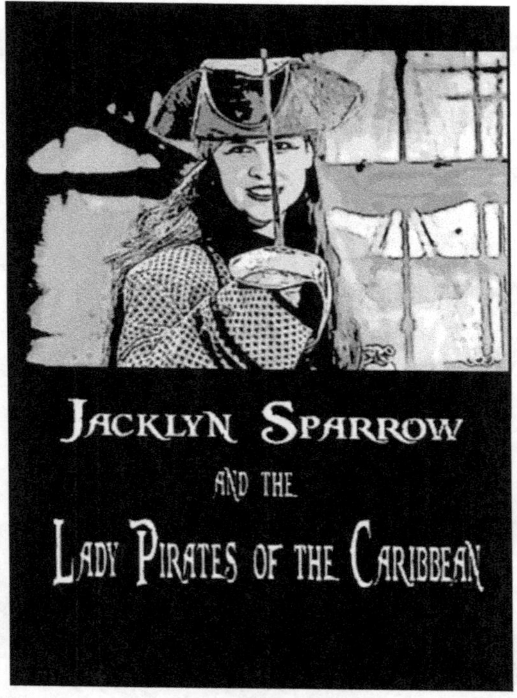

Why should the boys get to have all the fun?

Jacklyn Sparrow and the Lady Pirates of the Caribbean is our brand new swashbuckling pirate parody complete with bloodthirsty buccaneers in massive sword clanking battle scenes!! A giant wise cracking parrot named Polly!! Crazy obsessions with eye liner!! And just who is Robert, the Dreaded Phylum Porifera??

Of course the whole thing ends with a large celebration where everybody gets down with their bad selves!! It's fun for the whole family in this lampoon of everything you love about pirates!!!

NOW AVAILABLE!!!

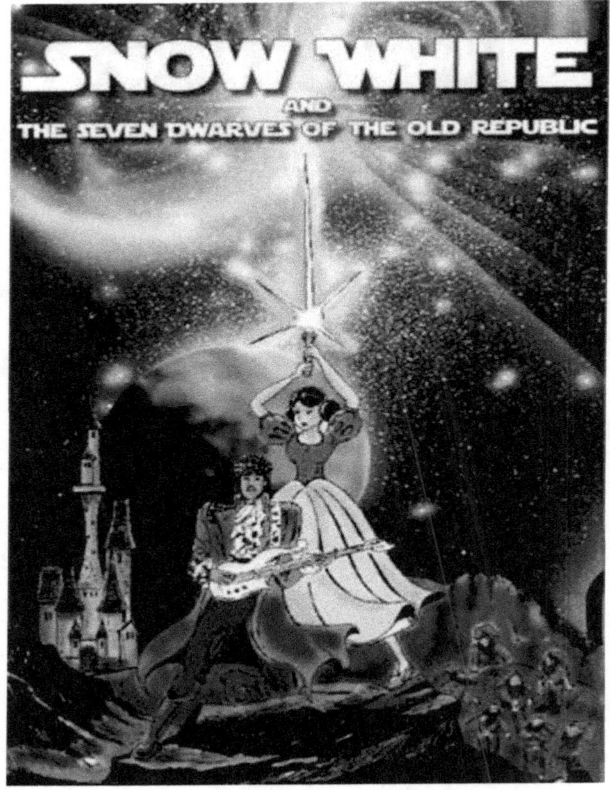

"May the Dwarf be with you!"

A wacky take on the classic fairy tale which will have audiences rolling in the floor with laughter!

What happens when you mix an articulate mirror, a conceited queen, a prince dressed in purple, seven little people with personality issues, a basket of kumquats and a little Star Wars for good measure?

Snow White and the Seven Dwarves of the Old Republic!

NOW AVAILABLE!!!

Declassified after 40 years!

On December 21, 1970, an impromptu meeting took place between the King of Rock and Roll and the Leader of the Free World.

Elvis Meets Nixon (Operation Wiggle) is a short comedy which offers one possible (and ultimately ridiculous) explanation of what happened during that meeting.

NOW AVAILABLE!!!

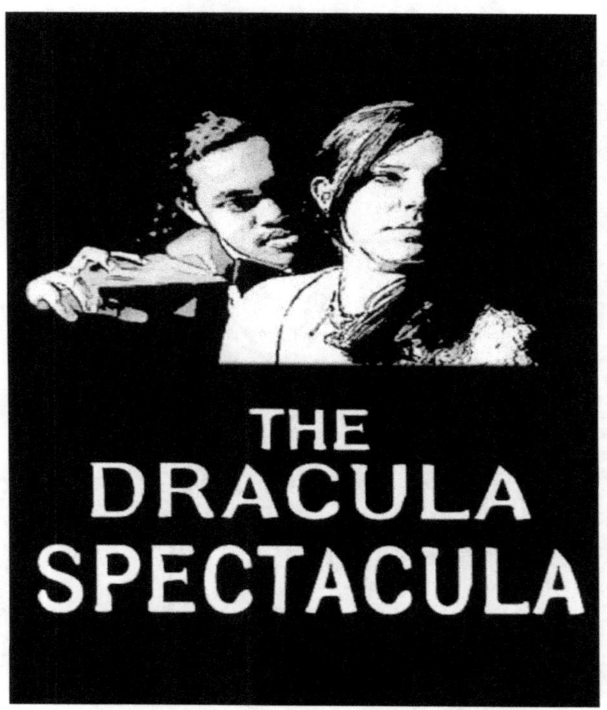

Count Dracula is bored. He's pretty much sucked Transylvania dry, and he's looking for a new challenge. So it's off to New York, New York! The Big Apple! The town that never sleeps...that'll pose a challenge for sure.
Dracula purchases The Carfax Theatre and decides to put on a big, flashy Broadway show...

THE DRACULA SPECTACULA!

Of course the Theatre just happens to be across the street from Dr. Seward's Mental Hospital where people have been mysteriously dying since The Count moved in.
Just a coincidence?
The play features a large cast of zany characters and is equal parts horror story and Broadway show spoof!

NOW AVAILABLE!!!

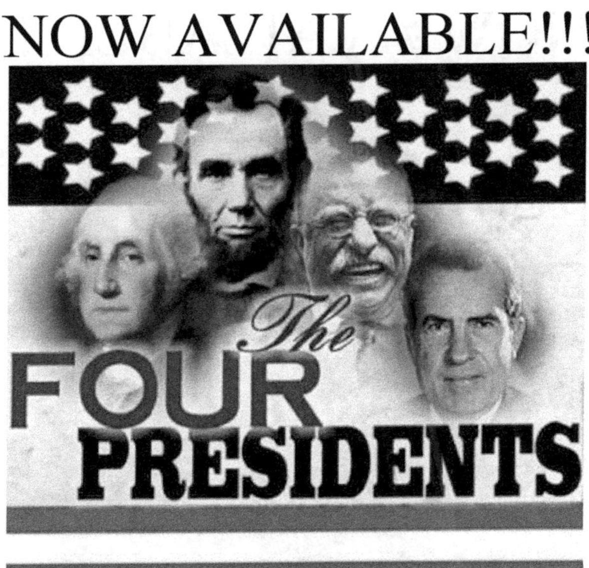

THE FOUR PRESIDENTS examines the lives and characters of four of the most colorful personalities to hold the office. Much of the dialogue comes from the Presidents' own words.

THE FARMER WHO WOULD BE KING presents George Washington through his own words, and the words of his biographer Mason Locke Weems. Was the father of our country a simple farmer who answered the call of his countrymen, or something more?

THE GREAT EMANCIPATOR is the story of a simple man. Born in the wilds of Kentucky and mostly self taught, Abraham Lincoln would someday be regarded as the greatest American who ever lived.

THE BULL MOOSE who occupied the White House 100 years ago was truly a man of action. Theodore Roosevelt was a father, author, rancher, sportsman, policeman, Rough Rider, cowboy, big game hunter, Governor of New York and eventually The President of the United States!

NIXON AND THE GHOSTS is a surreal drama with dialogue ripped straight from the headlines. On the night before his resignation, Nixon ponders his rise and fall, as the shadows themselves seem to come alive and he is confronted by the spirits of Presidents past!

NOW AVAILABLE!!!

NOW AVAILABLE!!!

Shorespeare is loosely based on a Midsummer Night's Dream. Shakespeare, with the help of Cupid, has landed at the Jersey Shore. Cupid inspires him to write a play about two New Jersey sweethearts, Cleo and Toni. Shakespeare is put off by their accent and way of talking, but decides to send the two teenagers on a course of true love. Toni and Cleo are determined to get married right after they graduate from high school, but in order to do so they must pass this course of true love that Cupid's pixies create and manipulate. As they travel along the boardwalk at the Jersey Shore, Cleo and Toni, meet a handful of historical figures disguised as the carnies. Confucius teaches Cleo the "Zen of Snoring", Charles Ponzi teaches them the importance of "White Lies", Leonardo Da Vinci shows them the "Art of Multitasking", and finally they meet Napolean who tries to help them to "Accept Shortcomings" of each other. After going through all these lessons, the sweethearts decide that marriage should wait, and Cupid is proud of Shakespeare who has finally reached out to the modern youth.

NOW AVAILABLE!!!

Everyone has heard the phrase, "it's the squeaky wheel that gets the oil," but how many people know the Back-story? The story begins in a kingdom far, far away over the rainbow – a kingdom called Spokend. This kingdom of wheels is a happy one for the gods have blessed the tiny hamlet with plentiful sunshine, water and most important –oil. Until a terrible drought starts to dry up all the oil supplies. What is to be done?

The powerful barons of industry and politicians decide to hold a meeting to decide how to solve the situation. Since Spokend is a democracy all the citizens come to the meeting but their voices are ignored – especially the voice of one of the poorer citizens of the community suffering from a squeak that can only be cured with oil, Spare Wheel and his wife Fifth Wheel. Despite Spare Wheel's desperate pleas for oil, he is ignored and sent home without any help or consideration.

Without oil, Spare Wheel's squeak becomes so bad he loses his job and his family starts to suffer when his sick leave and unemployment benefits run out. What is he to do? Spare Wheel and Fifth Wheel develop a scheme that uses the squeak to their advantage against the town magistrate Big Wheel who finally relents and gives over the oil. Thus, for years after in the town of Spokend citizens in need of help are told "It's the squeaky wheel that gets the oil."

www.ingramcontent.com/pod-product-compliance
Lightning Source LLC
LaVergne TN
LVHW051237080426
835513LV00016B/1644

* 9 7 8 0 6 9 2 4 4 8 9 3 9 *